Mike Trout: The Inspiring Story of One of Baseball's All-Stars

An Unauthorized Biography

By: Clayton (

D1165190

Table of Contents

Foreword

When others give you the nickname, "the Millville Meteor", you know you've done something impressive. That's the nickname of baseball center fielder, Mike Trout. Since being selected by the Los Angeles Angels in the first round of the 2009 MLB Draft, Trout has accumulated quite the stat sheet. At the time of this writing, he is an eight-time All-Star, three-time American League MVP, former American League Rookie of the Year, and seven-time Silver Slugger Award recipient. Bottom line: he is impressive to say the least, and a role model for young baseball fans. Thank you for purchasing *Mike Trout: The Inspiring Story of One of Baseball's All-Stars*. In this unauthorized biography, we will learn Mike Trout's incredible life story and impact on the game of baseball. Hope you enjoy and if you do, please do not forget to leave a review!

Also, check out my website at claytongeoffreys.com to join my exclusive list where I let you know about my latest books. To thank you for your purchase, you can go to my site to download a free copy of *33 Life Lessons: Success Principles, Career Advice & Habits of Successful People*. In the book, you'll learn from some of the greatest thought leaders of different industries on what it takes to become successful and how to live a great life.

Cheers,

Clayton Geoffreys

Visit me at www.claytongeoffreys.com

Introduction

Eight All-Star games. Three American League MVPs. Seven-time Silver Slugger Award winner. Four American League MVP runners-up. Six 30+ home run seasons in his young career.[i] When we talk about the greatest baseball players of the game today, the first name that comes to mind for any baseball connoisseur is Mike Trout of the Los Angeles Angels.

In 2012, when the then 20-year old Trout played his first full season in major league baseball, he gained the full respect of his teammates immediately. "He is one of the most dynamic players I have ever seen, if not the most," teammate Mark Trumbo acknowledged about him.[ii] Manager Mike Scioscia went even further. "He just does it in so many areas," Scioscia said. "He's doing it in the batter's box, he's doing it with the glove defensively, he's doing it with his legs."[ii]

And there is more.

Inspirational. Awe-inspiring. Team-player. Role model. Heroic. First-class. When we talk about model athletes for teenagers and young athletes today, not just in baseball but in any sport, there aren't enough adjectives to describe Mike Trout's incredible impact on the youth population.

Trout has become the idol baseball player for hundreds of thousands of children who want to "be just like Mike." (No, not that Mike. Baseball Mike, or as some know him, Philly Mike.). But Trout's success goes even further back than when people knew him as an All-Star baseball player and future Hall-of-Famer from the Los Angeles Angels of Anaheim. The star outfielder has not only astounded fans with his play on the field, but he has also impressed with what he has done off the field. His story has become an inspiration for thousands of little leaguers who are looking for the perfect athlete to idolize and be like.

"Behind the scenes, what you see is what you get," Trout's agent Craig Landis told MLB.com's Mark Feinsand. "Mike's one of the nicest, most polite and humble stars I've ever seen."[xxxiii]

"The regular-guy best player in the world. You don't see that a lot," Angels third baseman Zack Cozart said. "He's not trying to trick anybody. He's not fake. He's just being him. That's refreshing to see from a superstar."[xliv] Justin Upton added, "He's a dude first. That's all you can ask for—the big piece of your team to be a part of your team at the same time."[xliv]

And that is exactly who he is. Trout has become known for putting others first, from donating shoes to young athletes to visiting young children who are sick and need a pick-me-up or reason to smile. Mike will put baseball aside to help others. It is not for show. It is to make others feel good inside.

Respectful. Family-first. Humble. Passionate. Fun-loving. Phenom. Mike Trout is who he is today because of the way he was brought up by his parents, both teachers, Jeff and Debbie Trout. They raised a young boy and taught him to be respectful to everyone he comes across in life. They also didn't push baseball down his throat as most other parents would. Instead, they wanted Mike to find his passion, not force the passion upon him. As Mike grew up, he learned the essentials of life and how to be a humble and positive human being who had prodigious skills in baseball.

The story of Mike Trout is truly one of a kind. He is not your typical athlete who finds stardom. He is not the kind of athlete who changes as fame comes. He is not the type of person who walks around like he is the greatest thing since the radio or television was invented. He is the same well-mannered and gracious 28-year old that he was at six—just more grown-up, more mature, and more talented.

Trout was a proficient athlete from the day he was born. He had natural skills in baseball and basketball and played both at Millville High School in New Jersey. It was baseball, however, where his talents were cutting-edge. He was a star on the diamond and acquired the nickname, "The Millville Meteor." Other nicknames also followed him around, such as "God's Gift" and "The Prince Fish," soon to be changed to "King Fish 2.0."[iii]

While Trout would later become an outfielder, in high school he was a pitcher and shortstop. He broke the New Jersey record for home runs in a season and gained the reputation of being the fastest and strongest athlete by age 17.[iii]

Trout was drafted by the Angels with the 25th pick in the 2009 Major League Baseball Draft and debuted for the Arizona Angels later that year in Class A-League.[iv] He was not there long though, as he moved up the ladder. He played in the 2010 All-Star Futures Games and was named as "Baseball's Second-best Overall

Prospect." By age 19, he was named a Baseball America All-Star and a Topps Class A All-Star.[iv]

Things only got better from there for Trout. Just one year after debuting in the All-Star Futures Game as a member of the Class A-League, he was on the Los Angeles Angels roster. He made his debut for the Angels in July 2011 and hit his first of 285 home runs (as of March 2020) against the Orioles. That year, he was named Baseball's Minor League Player of the Year and made the Minor League All-Star Team.

In 2012, he became a regular starter for the Angels. It was not long before he made the 24 teams that drafted before the Angels in 2009 regret not drafting him. Trout was Rookie of the Month four times in 2012 and led the league in several different categories, including runs, batting average, and stolen bases. He won the BBWAA Jackie Robinson Rookie of the Year Award by a unanimous vote. Many thought he was deserving of American League MVP, especially because of his stellar outfield play, but he finished second in that category to Miguel Cabrera of the Tigers.[iv]

From there, Trout's career only got better. He won his first of four American League MVPs in 2014 and has been on the All-Star Team every year since. While many players shine early in their careers and then slowly run out of steam, it has only picked up for Trout. He has batted over or just shy of .300 each of the last three seasons (2017, 2018, 2019) and just finished 2019 with a career-high 45-home run season, earning his fourth MVP Award.[v]

Trout has been such a positive influence on the game. The superstar has reminded people that there are still good people in sports, people with a heart who have talent. He has illustrated the same respect, the same humility, and the same competitiveness as he did as a young boy growing up on the baseball diamond. Mike has always wanted to be the best, but he didn't let that affect his personality in any way. His high school teammates loved him, and his coach had nothing but respect for him.

Mike Trout is truly a special athlete. All young ball players need to know his story. They need to know how to act while growing up in the game. They need to know that respect and humility still hold an important place in society. They need to know that hard work pays off in the end and rewards come with it. They need to know what it is like to be like Mike Trout.

If there is any baseball player to emulate, he is the guy.

Chapter 1: Early Life and Childhood

Michael Nelson Trout was born on August 7, 1991, in Vineland, N.J. and raised in Millville, N.J by his parents, Jeff and Debbie. His passion for baseball came from his father, who played for the Minnesota Twins. Unfortunately, Jeff Trout had to retire after just four years in the minor leagues due to an onslaught of injuries, particularly to his knee.

Mike was the youngest of three children and grew up a die-hard Philadelphia Phillies fan. Living less than an hour from Phillies Stadium, he got the opportunity to go to a few Phillies games as a kid, including the 2008 World Series against the Tampa Bay Rays.

The Trouts grew up in a middle-class environment in New Jersey. Mike's parents taught Mike, his brother Tyler, and sister Teal, a lot of things, most notably to be respectful to everyone they come across and to have balance in their lives.

"We wanted Mike to put victories and losses in perspective," Debbie Trout recalled in an interview she did with the *Huffington Post*. "We told him to be a good person, and everything else will just take care of itself. Be kind and be respectful."[viii]

Mike did just that. He always referred to his parents' friends as Mr. and Mrs., not just as a child, but also as an adult, according to his mother. It is something, unfortunately, you don't hear very often these days. Treat others with respect, no matter who they are, whether they are a friend or an enemy. That is how you gain respect back.

One thing most families don't do in society today is to eat together as a family. That was not the case with the Trouts. They ate dinner together at least five nights a week, even if it was on the way to a baseball game or practice. Sometimes it would be just pizza in the car. But they felt one of the most important and healthy things a family could adhere to was just being together and socializing. The Trouts would just talk. It didn't matter what it was, they wanted to communicate as a family, especially on holidays. When Thanksgiving came, that phone was put away in the Trout household. You didn't dare take it out. It was a day for family.[viii]

The Trouts had strict rules for their children, but one rule they never imposed was forcing them to do an activity or play a sport they didn't want to take part in. It was Jeff's hope the boys would love playing baseball, but he didn't pressure them into it. Jeff and Debbie felt that, as long as the kids were respectful to them and others, they could just enjoy themselves.

"We let them be kids," Debbie said. "A lot of these parents take promising kids and don't let them have a life beyond baseball. We let them go out with their friends and go fishing and play other sports. Some parents don't let their kids put down a ball all year-round and that was not what we wanted to do at all."[viii]

However, the Trouts never needed to force baseball upon Mike. He found the game on his own. As a young boy, Mike used to shag baseballs for the Millville High School baseball team and then became the bat boy for them while his father coached. Even as a young boy, he showed tremendous athletic ability, wowing the players with some of his catches while shagging balls with the high school boys.[v] He illustrated his passion for the game early.

Mike's involvement early on in his childhood got him recognized. It is something that is important for all young athletes to learn. You don't realize it many times when you are young, but being around others in the game at an early age raises eyes in a good way. They find out who you are. It shows your passion, and that along with talent is something all coaches look for in kids at an early age. This played a role with Mike Trout. As he got involved in more activities involving baseball, coaches began to pay attention more and more.

No doubt, Mike definitely loved baseball. His parents reminisce about how he used to sleep in his T-ball uniform on the day of games.[viii] That was all he would talk about at home and all he wanted to wear. It was his passion. It was becoming his life more and more as he grew older.

Craig Atkinson was the Trout's neighbor and recalled hearing the sound "ping" outside of his home every time he sat down to eat dinner with his family. He would look outside and there was five-year-old Mike Trout, known as Mikey by Atkinson, hitting rocks with his aluminum bat.[xl]

"It would go on for hours," Atkinson told *NJ Monthly*.[xl]

Trout's other neighbor was Tim Shannon, the mayor of Millville. He and Atkinson grew up watching Mike hit balls outside and knew from the time he was a little boy that he was something special.

No matter how much baseball took over his life, Mike was extremely appreciative of his parents and grateful towards them. He gives a lot of his accolades today in baseball to how his parents raised him and the lessons they taught him as a child.

"I couldn't ask for better parents," Mike said. "From day one, my dad told me if he had to force me to do something, he didn't want me to do it. I just always wanted to play baseball. I didn't want to be that cocky kid. I just wanted to go out there and play. I had fun playing. You just go out there and play the game every day."[viii]

At first, however, Mike wanted to be a teacher when he was growing up, just like his parents were. When he was growing up, his parents always taught him to have a backup plan, a Plan B, in case Plan A didn't work out. Mike's primary plan was first to become a teacher, which became Plan B sooner rather than later when baseball became his passion.[viii]

He always had a plan, though. He never put all his eggs in one basket. He kept his mind organized with what he wanted to do, and if his first goal didn't pan out, he had a backup plan. You need to have an open mind growing up because life throws you curveballs, and you just never know what it will throw your way. Fortunately for Mike, Plan A would work out. However, it does not work that way for every star athlete.

Mike was always ahead of the game when playing at a young age. He was obsessed with baseball by the age of eight and was light-years ahead of his teammates on the field. He had the talent of a high school baseball player when he was only in the third grade. According to his baseball coach in Ripken Little League, Mike Kavanagh, "Mike was better than the league of 12-year-olds when he was just 9."[vii]

According to Mayor Shannon, he and Atkinson used to go watch Mike all the time and were just amazed at the things he did. He was hitting monster home runs as a little leaguer against big-league competition.[xl] There were not enough adjectives to describe the things he was doing so young.

Mike was able to develop such a talent in the game because of his father. Jeff Trout had already retired by the time he was raising his children and he helped Mike develop fast instincts and incredible skills at the plate and on the field. Mike was a righty but hit lefty in his early days. While Mike is an outfielder today, he was the best pitcher and shortstop in his Little League. Additionally, he was the fastest kid in the league, running from the batter's box to first base in under four seconds.[iv]

It didn't take long for Mike's dad, Jeff, to realize the prodigy he had. When Mike was just a little boy, he was doing superhuman things.

"Mike's near shortstop, this kid hits a line drive up the middle," Jeff recalled. "Mike takes two steps to his left, dives parallel to the ground, and catches it. I'll never forget the look Debbie and I gave each other. It was a jaw-dropper. I wish I had it on video."[ix]

Like Debbie, Jeff felt it was important not to push Mike too much in baseball. He saw what other parents had done to their kids and how it had ruined them. He didn't want Mike to be a youth sports burnout. Jeff felt it was more important for him to just enjoy the game and let the process take care of itself. According to Jeff, he wanted to keep it simple. Just play, have fun, be a team player, take care of the body, play with passion, and always play to win.

It is something that not just the Trouts, but many great athletes' parents have in common. Pushing a kid too hard too early on can burn them out. While, yes, many parents are a little tougher on their kids' practice and playing schedules than Jeff and Debbie were, they wanted them to have their freedom and just enjoy childhood. It was a vital part of the early process.

However, that was not the most important thing the Trouts taught their children.

"Do well in school," Jeff told his kids.[ix]

Mike's parents wanted their kids to have fun, but other priorities came first, such as school. Jeff and Debbie focused more on being tough with their children in the most important areas, such as learning how to treat others with respect and making sure they got good grades. School always came first. You can't play in high school or college if you do not have good grades. Most every school restricts that. It was not a problem with Mike because his parents drilled home the importance of maintaining good grades. And if you do not treat your teachers and coaches with respect, it can prevent your baseball career from moving forward.

While there was the athletic side of Mike that we already know about, there were other sides of him that many people do not know. He was a prankster as a child, along with his older brother Tyler, and loved to play practical jokes on others, including his own family members.

"I remember growing up, one time we put a walkie-talkie on my grandmother's dog and sent him into her house and we were talking to her through the walkie-talkie," Tyler recalled to *USA Today* in an interview. "She's looking at the dog thinking, 'Is this dog really...' and we're (Mike and I) watching through the window laughing uncontrollably."[vi] Tyler then said that his grandmother started responding back to the dog.

Ironically enough, the prankster got his nickname from a prank that was pulled on him during his high school playing days. Someone edited his Wikipedia article and put the nickname "Millville Meteor" on there and the name caught on.[vi]

Mike and his brother Tyler were really close growing up. Not only did they play pranks on others and each other, but they also played games together, sometimes getting themselves in trouble unintentionally. The two would regularly go to the Cumberland County Fair and play games, including one where they would knock over milk bottles stacked in a pyramid with a baseball.

Unfortunately, Mike was not only good at it—he was *too* good. Mike was banned from playing the game after the fair realized he was winning too much for their liking and hurting business. "He was knocking them down all the time and taking all the prizes," Terry Pangbum of the Cumberland County Fair stated.[vi] According to his brother Tyler, Mike was furious with the fair's decision.

Mike's competitiveness sometimes got the best of him, and his parents had to give him a talking to. When he was pitching for the town championship when he was eight years old, his team lost 1-0. Mike was so upset that he didn't want to go out and accept the second-place trophy. However, his parents would not accept that outcome.

"I told him, 'If you don't go out there and accept that trophy, you are not playing baseball ever again,'" Debbie recollected. "He then went out there to accept the second-place trophy and stomped back."[viii] While Mike was upset, Debbie believed it was a critical moment in his life. "He knew he had to hang with it, that you come in second place sometimes. You have to accept it."[viii]

It was a valuable lesson; sometimes in order to move forward, you need to take a small step back. Life isn't always going to be a victory. There will be moments when others will have better days than you. You have to accept that. It is how you learn from the defeat that makes you a better person.

In the end, Jeff and Debbie proved to be exemplary parents for Mike. The lessons they taught him carried with him throughout his life, not just in childhood, but in high school, the minor leagues, and beyond. They raised him the way any parent should raise their boys.

Because of their parenthood, Mike is one of the most respected and idolized athletes in the game today by the younger population.

"Our goal was to develop our child into a good all-around human being so he could enjoy life with baseball and beyond baseball," Jeff explained. "As a parent, that is your job. Not to raise the greatest player, but instead to raise a great person. If a sport is what they excel at, then it is your job to give them every opportunity to excel."[ix]

Mike's Idol

When Mike was growing up, there was no one he looked up to more than Derek Jeter. While the Phillies were his favorite team, Jeter was his idol, so much so that he wore Number 2 in Little League because of the legendary Yankees shortstop who at the time was in his prime.

Jeter, in Trout's mind, was the perfect player to emulate—a superstar athlete who showed humility and grace on *and* off the field. A man who illustrated consistency, meaning he didn't let downswings in the game or his life change who he was. What you saw was what you got. It was a reputation that would inspire Mike Trout as he grew up in the game. Mike wanted to play shortstop like Jeter, which he did, and try to carry the same grace and respect for the game that his idol showed.

Mike loved watching baseball as a kid. Despite his love for the Phillies, he always wanted to watch the Yankees play whenever they were on television just so he could see Derek Jeter. He didn't care about anyone else. He just wanted to see the player he idolized and worshipped.

Maybe one of the best stories in baseball comes when Mike was older and a member of the Los Angeles Angels. He got to play against Derek Jeter before the great shortstop retired. Standing on second base during a game in 2011, Trout looked over at Jeter and asked him for an autograph.

"I was so nervous and so starstruck," Trout told Dan Patrick in an interview on his radio show.[xii] Trout could not recall how Jeter responded because he was in shock, just like you would be if you ran into your hero in person, but he did get what he asked for. Before the series ended, Jeter gave Trout a signed baseball. It is a moment Trout would never forget. It was something that he had always dreamed of as a little boy. According to Trout, it was one of the best moments of his life.[xiii]

It is a testament that dreams can come true. This was something that Mike thought of all the time as a little kid, that he would be standing next to the player that he wanted to be like when he was older. Mike got his wish but he didn't let that moment be the peak of his career. Better things were to come from then on.

Chapter 2: High School Career

"On a list of who my hardest workers have been, he (Mike Trout) was the hardest worker." – Roy Hallenbeck, manager for Mike Trout at Millville High School [x]

There was much anticipation before Mike Trout stepped onto the Millville Thunderbolts baseball field for the first time. Mike's dad, Jeff, was already a fixture at the school long before anyone knew who Mike was. He was a history teacher and former baseball coach at the school. After his baseball career ended, he got into the profession, like his wife, shortly before Mike was even born. When Mike was only six years old, he would come to practices to help out with the team, even serving as the team's batboy. Jeff, however, did not coach Mike in high school. Rather, he felt it better to not put pressure on him and stay out of the way while Mike developed.

Jeff knew Mike already had a lot of pressure on him. He felt if he coached him in high school, it would only add to that pressure. So, he wanted to let other instructors work with Mike while he stayed out of the way.[xii] Mike never said so publicly, but many young players are like that. They do not feel comfortable with their mother or father getting directly involved and coaching them. It really does add pressure. Many parents understand this and it is why they step out of the way.

Mike was already making a name for himself on the diamond before he got to Millville. At age 14, he was playing for the Tri-State Arsenal travel baseball team. He continued to play travel baseball during his tenure in high school and played in the Perfect Game WWBA Baseball Championships in Florida in 2007 and 2008.

Before his first day at school, Coach Hallenbeck was well aware of who Mike Trout was, as was pretty much the entire baseball team. Word had spread of just how talented this kid was. Hallenbeck had a meeting with Mike and his dad before the season began to talk about the team and expectations. Hallenbeck recalls coming away from that meeting incredibly impressed with Mike as a person.

"This was a humble and respectful kid who was as competitive as anyone you will ever meet," Hallenbeck said. "That's a rarity. You could tell this was a special player from day one."[x]

Trout's exceptional childhood talents earned him a spot on the Millville High School Varsity Team as a freshman. On the first day, he was arguably already the most talented player on the team. However, unlike many high school athletes who come in cocky and not feeling the need to put in as much effort, Trout was the opposite. He was eager to learn and push himself to be better, no matter how much talent he already had. The last adjective any one of his teammates would use for him was "arrogant."

"I think it would have been different if I had come up and been this cocky little kid, talking smack to people," Mike said. "That's not who I wanted to be, though. That's not me."[viii]

Mike wanted to be the humble and respectful guy and he instantly made friends on the team and earned their respect because of how he held himself as an athlete and a person. He felt it was an important lesson in life for others to follow and soon youngsters would be looking up to that part of Mike Trout. Be someone others want to be like, not someone that people fear talking to, are intimidated by, or are turned off by.

While Mike is known now for his outfield skills, he didn't play it growing up or in high school. He was a star pitcher for Millville as well as a shortstop just like his idol, Derek Jeter. Hallenbeck used him very sparingly in the outfield until his senior season when he began playing it full-time.[x]

Mike was big in stature growing up and only increased in size in high school. He grew to over six feet tall and surpassed 200 pounds by his senior year. There was no doubt a lot of power behind the big frame of Mike Trout, but there was also a lot of speed. Mike was one of the fastest, if not *the* fastest, guy on the team.

"Every high school kid makes a big jump at some point from one offseason to the next," Hallenbeck explained to *MLB.com*. "That's just their growth spurt. Mike did it every year. It was like, 'Are you kidding me? Where's the plateau?' He just never hit it."[xi]

Mike didn't want to be just good at Millville; he wanted to be the best. In order to achieve that, he needed to surpass someone he was very familiar with—his father. Jeff Trout held all the Millville High School baseball records, from batting average to hits to home runs. Beginning his freshman year, Mike's talent was recognized by scouts, including Greg Morhardt, the Los Angeles Angels scout who oversaw the Northeast region of the country.

Morhardt had a history with Mike's father, Jeff. They both played together in the minor leagues with the Twins. According to Morhardt, he had never in his life witnessed a faster and stronger 17-year-old than Mike Trout.

"When I saw this phenom, I asked what his name was, and someone said, 'Mike Trout.' I thought for a few seconds and it all of a sudden hit me that I played with Jeff Trout and recalled he went to school at Millville," Morhardt told *ESPN's* Buster Olney. "I thought, 'Is there a connection?' I soon found out there was."[xii]

Mike put up impressive numbers all four years but really began to shine during his third year. That year, he threw a no-hitter against Egg Harbor Township High School. He helped lead the Thunderbolts to the state playoffs that year, but they were defeated by Cherry Hill East High School.

During his senior year, he was shifted to the outfield and it was then that he broke the records that were set by his father. In 81 at-bats that year, he hit 18 home runs, a New Jersey high school record. He posted a .531 batting average, a school record, and had 20 steals.

Teams were afraid to face him. Mike broke a record for most times intentionally walked in high school, including an infamous one that became a legend in all of New Jersey and beyond.

In the South Jersey Group 4 Quarterfinals, Cherry Hill East manager Erik Radbill had one simple strategy in that game: "Don't let Mike Trout beat us."[xxxix] You could say he "unintentionally" did that. Cherry Hill East intentionally walked Mike Trout three times in that game, including once when the bases were already loaded. Yes, they sacrificed a run just so they would not have to face him.[xxxix]

"He (Mike) was electric, even as a junior," Mike Edwards, former Millville assistant coach said. "He did things on a baseball field that you hadn't seen up to that point and really, quite honestly, you really haven't seen afterward. He was different."[xxix]

Yes, he was different. Mike enjoyed that, though. As a baseball player, you do not want to be the same as everyone else. You hear the phrase, "Don't be the next Babe Ruth. Be the first 'You.'" Trout wanted to be the first Trout. He wanted to have his own style, his own way of carrying himself, his own place in the game. Other than maybe Derek Jeter for a short time as a kid, he didn't want to be like anyone else. He wanted to just be himself. He wanted to be this big kid who had incredible speed mixed with amazing power and a side of humility and respect to go with it.

However, while those in the Northeast knew who he was, many around the nation didn't. Unfortunately, the way New Jersey works, baseball seasons are short. He didn't get the national exposure other high school kids were getting because there isn't much of a season thanks to the reduced spring in the Northeast. When he was not playing baseball, working on his studies, or spending time with his friends and family, Mike was on the hardcourt playing basketball.

"Mikey just loved competition," Mayor Shannon said. "In basketball, the rougher it got under the boards, the more Mikey thrived. He enjoyed that. He really thrived against that competition, especially going against the better players. It was almost like he stepped up his game."[xl]

Basketball would eventually take a back seat, however, as Mike focused more and more on a career in baseball after he left Millville.

The One That Got Away

Mike was being targeted by many colleges to play baseball for them. East Carolina University baseball coach Billy Godwin wanted his skills badly. He noticed the prodigy at 16 years old and was astounded by his speed, power, and raw athleticism. He pushed hard for Trout to come to the university.[xiv]

In July 2008, Trout committed to play for the East Carolina Pirates and in November 2018, he was officially listed on the Pirates roster to play for the team in the 2009-10 season. In the press release, Godwin said about Trout, "Mike is one of the best athletes I have seen on the diamond and will go into his senior year as one of the top outfielders in the country. He has tremendous speed and power and will be a mainstay in the outfield and the top half of our lineup during his tenure as a Pirate."[xiv]

While Godwin was as excited as any coach in the country to get Mike's services, a player he saw as one of the greatest he had ever seen, he was nervous he was going to lose him to the major leagues. Mike was shooting up draft boards during his senior year. While some players get drafted and still decide to forego the big leagues to play in college, if they are drafted in the first round, they almost always forego college because of the salary that they get offered as well as the opportunity. This had Godwin worried.

"Going into the fall, I thought he was very, very talented, probably a third-to-seventh round pick, maybe," Godwin said. "Then I saw him play in the spring. Forget it. There was no shot. This guy was a first-rounder, easy."[xiv] Godwin never saw an athletic specimen like what he saw in Trout.

During the draft, Trout fell, but not far enough. He was drafted by the Los Angeles Angels of Anaheim in the first round of the 2009 Major League Baseball Draft with the 25th pick. Trout signed for a $1.2 million signing bonus and committed to playing minor league ball with the Angels.

Godwin lost his dream player. And like any college baseball coach who lost their dream player to the majors, Godwin always wonders what it would have been like to have Trout as a part of their team. It would have probably helped shape Godwin's career as a coach, having an athlete Mike Trout play college baseball for him. But it just was not meant to be. It was "the one that got away."

However, no one could blame Mike Trout. Any young athlete who gets a chance at the major leagues after being drafted in the first round cannot pass up that opportunity. Once players start going in the third round and higher, there is the possibility, and sometimes likelihood, that they'll choose college over the pros. But not after the first round. Mike had too much talent to ignore what the Angels were offering him.

So just like that, Mike was on his way to the start of his professional career.

Chapter 3: Minor League Career

"Give me something on Mike Trout. Just one thing...Please!"– Scott Servais, Angels scouting assistant, 2005-2012[xv]

There had to be a weakness. There had to be a flaw. There had to be a kryptonite in Mike Trout.

"Well, he slugs almost .900 in almost every area of the strike zone," Scott Servais said. "However, there's this one little, tiny area of the strike zone way up and away where he slugs only .400." [xv]

Twenty-four teams passed on Mike Trout in the 2009 Major League Baseball Draft. It was not until the 25th pick, a compensatory pick that the Los Angeles Angels got from the Yankees for the trade of Mark Teixeira, where Trout was selected. Within a few years' time, Trout would make the 23 teams that picked ahead of them (the Angels also picked 24th) sorry.

The Angels were beyond ecstatic that Mike fell to them at number 25. They, and all of the scouts and personnel that knew Mike best, were also stunned. The Angels were not sure if he would be there, but somehow, he was. Like any star athlete starting out, there is optimism, but there is also doubt. Even with the great ones. So many first-round draft picks come in with loads of promise but never get out of the minor leagues. Ever see the movie *Moneyball*? The Billy Bean story is exactly that. Sometimes players do not make the majors because of injury. Sometimes it is because they were misevaluated. Sometimes the new life and freedom just get the best of them, especially the postgame nightlife. Sometimes their egos get in the way and it quickly gets put in check when things go wrong.

So, even with the very promising Mike Trout, there was skepticism. When scouts look for the next great thing, they do not necessarily look for the highlights and great characteristics of an athlete. They look for the bad, the thing that could hinder their career, and then assess whether it can be fixed or not.

The identifiable weakness in Trout really had nothing to do with him, in general, but rather the recent history of New Jersey kids failing in the minor leagues. It went back to Mike's dad, Jeff, who never made it past AA ball, although the talent in him was there; injury held him back. There was a run of recent New Jersey first-round picks seen as "can't miss stars" who flopped or had season-ending injuries and never made it to the major league level. There was also the fact that bad weather forced Millville not to play a lot of games in 2009 and scouts questioned Mike's overwhelming size for a kid at 18. Mike also didn't play in a lot of big showcase events nationwide as some high school phenoms did. Some of these reasons cast doubt among many general managers in drafting New Jersey super kid Mike Trout in the first round.[xvi] Little did these general managers know that they were about to be proved dead wrong in their suppositions about Mike.

When Mike stepped onto the field for his first minor league game with the Arizona Angels, the club's Rookie A-League team, there were not many fans in attendance. Mike had himself a heck of a debut, though. He reached base six times and eyebrows started to raise from the start. After he was done with Rookie A-Ball, he finished with a .360 batting average with 25 RBIs in 164 at-bats.[i] Mike was quickly on his way to Cedar Rapids, Iowa to play regular A-ball.

Some players can spend a year, two years, or even more with a minor league team. Some go back and forth as they go through streaks and slumps. For Mike, this definitely was not the case. Once he got to Cedar Rapids, it was like Ken Miles at the 24 Hours of Le Mans in *Ford vs. Ferrari*. He just kept hitting a new gear and new level and passing other men left and right on his way to the finish line. He was rising, just like his idol, Derek Jeter.

It was in Cedar Rapids with the Kernels where Mike Trout's career really took off and the Angels' front office truly began to pay attention. Trout played 81 games with the Kernels, hitting .362 with 6 home runs and 39 RBIs.[i] He was named to the Midwest League All-Star Team where he started center field. He was then asked to play in the XM All-Star Futures Game in Anaheim, an event that allows fans to get a closer look at the minor league players who could be playing with the major league club in a few years' time. Mike led the Midwest League in four categories before heading off to Rancho Cucamonga for A+-League ball: batting average (.362), runs scored (76), stolen bases (45), and hits (113). He was named the Midwest League MVP that season.[iv]

Mike continued to advance his way through the minor leagues. After hitting .362 and hitting the cover off the ball to start the season in A-ball in Cedar Rapids, he went to Rancho Cucamonga and hit .306 before going to AA and playing for the Arkansas Travelers, where he hit .326 and hit 11 home runs in 353 at-bats.[i] Then, when Peter Bourjos of the Los Angeles Angels went on the disabled list, Mike Trout got a call. *The* call.

He was headed to Anaheim.

Not Quite Ready

Many baseball players get that taste of the major leagues for the first time. It is unlike any other. The feeling of playing for your team at the top level, going to stadiums filled with 50,000+ fans, all their eyes squarely on you. You know in their minds they're saying, "This could be the next great legend in the game!" It can be daunting and overwhelming. For some who have been around the game for a while, they make the best of their opportunity. For Mike Trout, who was still young and not even old enough to drink beer yet, it was a sign he just was not quite ready.

Justin Hollander, the Angels scouting and player development assistant at the time, recalled the first day Mike Trout walked into the locker room for the Angels. "It was almost like the first day of the regular season or the first day of the playoffs," Hollander told Ben Lindbergh of *The Ringer*. "There was a buzz in the hallway unlike any other."[xvi]

Word spread quickly on Mike Trout. He was advancing through the minor leagues faster than any Angel before him and this young kid was now donning an Angels uniform at such a young age. The players knew he had to be good. He had to be phenomenal. He had to be the kid who would win this team a World Series one day. Those kinds of expectations would be tough on any kid.

Before Trout got called up, though, there was concern among the scouts and player development coaches. Abe Flores, the Angels director of player development at the time, was optimistic yet concerned. According to

Flores, there was some worry with his swing when he first started rookie league ball in that he had too steep a swing. However, that was fixed early on and his numbers indicated progression. But concerns still lingered.

Flores was right in that you need to be careful with young prospects. Flores felt it was important to take your time because if they come up too early and experience failure, they begin to question their ability. That is the risk young athletes run into when they get to this level. Can they adjust to bigger moments? Can they rise to the occasion? But most importantly, how do they react when their confidence takes a hit and things do not go so well.

Baseball is such a confidence sport, a mental game as much as a physical game. It can ruin careers. Slumps can last days, then weeks, then months, then careers. It can mentally destroy you. The minute you begin to doubt your ability, it is a hard climb back up that ladder. It is why so many teams do not elevate rookies and young stars to the major leagues right away. They are very careful because if they do bring them up too fast and they experience failure at the top level, it can end their careers.

This is what Trout, and any young prospect coming up, has to deal with. Not every day is going to be sunny. Can you overcome the bad moments and stop a slide from escalating out of control when it is going downhill fast? This is how Mike Trout became a star. He knew how to deal with setbacks.

Eddie Bane was the Angels amateur scouting director and played a big role in the team drafting Trout. Trout was just behind Stephen Strasburg on his personal draft preference list.[xvi] Bane admits to this very day he was wrong on that list, saying Trout should have been number one. Bane recalls just how amazed he was at Trout's athletic ability. He recalled how he ran to first base in under four seconds in the Futures All-Star

Game three times. "Everybody talks about pushing them too fast, but one of the hardest parts about scouting is not pushing them fast enough when they're ready, when they're a different bird," Bane said.[xvi]

The Angels didn't want to continue to waste him against minor league pitching, and they had seen enough that they were ready to take the next step and promote him two levels. And so it was. On July 8, 2011, Mike Trout would be the youngest to ever don a Los Angeles Angels uniform since Andy Hassler in 1971.[xvi]

Trout walked onto the field for the first time as an Angel that day and left disappointed. He went 0-for-3, and through his first nine games and 30 at-bats, he had just four hits and one extra-base hit, a double. It was not the start he had envisioned to his major league career.

However, things began to turn around for Trout after the jitters went away. "For a two-week stretch there, he had a .800 OPS and he was doing all of the things you would expect Mike Trout to be doing," Hollander said.[xvi] During that stretch, Trout hit .356 and belted five home runs. By September 3rd, his OPS was up to .861.

He was tearing it up so much during that two-week stretch, it appeared as if Mike Trout would never see the minor leagues again.

Then came the slump. And it was bad.

In his next 50 plate appearances, Trout hit .146 and struck out 17 times. His slugging percentage and on-base percentage were under .200 and he ended the season with a batting average of .220 in the major leagues.[xvi]

Trout was sent back to Scottsdale to play for Arizona's fall league team and he struggled there as well, posting a .245 average in 106 at-bats. Worse, he had 33 strikeouts, meaning he was striking out an average of once every three at-bats. Some may have questioned whether it was a confidence problem, but many believed fatigue was a major factor. According to Hollander, Trout was "already dead tired" by that time and needed the break before starting the 2012 season. He hadn't yet adapted to the longer seasons. Remember, in New Jersey, a long high school season was 18 games. The minor leagues are 140 games and major leagues are 162, not counting the postseason.

Scott Servais began to become nervous about Trout's potential when he went to Arizona and saw Trout for the first time. However, Jerry Dipoto reassured him. "Scott, don't worry," Dipoto said. "This guy is going to be the next big thing in our sport."[xvi]

When 2012 began, the Angels decided to start Mike in AAA ball in Salt Lake City, hoping to regain his form.

He did more than regain his form. He took his game to a level no one had ever seen before.

The Comeback

"But it ain't about how hard you hit. It's about how hard you can get hit and keep moving forward; how much you can take and keep moving forward. That's how winning is done! Now if you know what you're worth, then go out and get what you're worth, but you gotta be willing to take the hits, and not pointing fingers saying you ain't where you wanna be because of him, or her, or anybody." – Rocky Balboa[xviii]

It is such an important lesson in life. The world is not all sunshine and rainbows. There are dark days, especially for baseball players. Remember, they fail more than they succeed at the plate, failing more than 7 times out of 10 for most ballplayers. However, it is how you bounce back from those failures that define you.

For the first time, Mike Trout had experienced a setback. A disappointing beginning with the Angels major league team by his standards and then a rough close with the Arizona Fall Team. However, Mike was not going to let that be the last time he saw Angels Stadium. There were two ways he could have taken his rough debut with the Angels. He could let it get to him and slide down like so many other major league players have done before him. Or he could use it as fuel, as motivation to get back to that level and prove to everyone that he is the next great player in the Angels organization.

Like the Rocky Balboa quote, Mike got hit, and he was ready to hit back.

The Angels had plans for him to make it back to Anaheim, and they started him off in AAA ball in Salt Lake City. Mike absolutely crushed the ball for his first 20 games of the AAA season. In 77 at-bats, Mike hit .403, scored 21 runs, and stole 6 bases. He put up a slugging percentage of .623 and walked 11 times.[i] It was clear that he was refreshed from the offseason break and was able to regroup just fine.

In late April, when Bobby Abreu was released by the Angels, they called up Mike Trout again, hoping for better results out of him the second time around. They were about to get them.

Mike was not as nervous the second go-round. He had gotten his punch in the gut the summer before and was ready for what the major leagues had to give him. He didn't want to go back; he was ready this time to stay at the top and help the team win games. It didn't take long for that to happen.

On April 28, 2012, Mike Trout was about to become a name that would become synonymous with major league baseball for years to come.

Chapter 4: Major League Career

Rookie Season

When it comes to wins above replacement, a formula that weighs a player's overall contribution to the team in terms of wins and losses, you would hope to be around four or five wins in the positive. Most seasons, that gets you ranked pretty high as a player. In 2012, Mike Trout's was 10.5 games—more than two runs above the next highest-ranked player that season, Robinson Cano.[xvii]

When Mike Trout was called up from AAA ball in Salt Lake City and donned the Angels uniform once again, there was a different sort of buzz in the air. A year ago, there was a sense that it may have been too early to judge Mike and that he was tired and not quite ready for the spotlight. However, this time, it felt different. Mike was destroying the ball in AAA ball and came in with a different confidence and swag about him than he did the year before. He was also more relaxed and refreshed, whereas the previous year his body was tiring out and needed a rest. This time, he was determined to make the best of his opportunity and let the league know he was not a fluke.

However, once again his start with the Angels was not so glorious. Trout began his second stint in the majors in Cleveland, and it didn't go well. In his first game back on the major league roster, Mike went 0-for-4 with a strikeout. The next night at the same ballpark, he went 0-for-3, marking an 0-for-7 opening road trip. As he headed back to Los Angeles to begin his first home series of the season, murmurs from Angels fans had begun. The whispers of "here we go again" could be sensed going on inside the heads of fans. Was this yet another Angels phenom bust? Another Jersey boy who reached his peak in the minors? Another Trout whose career would end short?

But just as those doubts started to creep into the minds of fans, they were quickly erased in front of their very eyes. The Angels were about to start the first game of a three-game series against the Minnesota Twins at home. The first game was the one that changed Mike Trout forever.

Mike got a hit in that game, going 1-for-4. The next night, he was 1-for-3 with a stolen base. Then it was a two-hit night against the Blue Jays. By the middle of May, just a few weeks into his rookie season, Trout was hitting .338 with hits in 12 out of 16 games. He hit his first home run on May 7th against the Blue Jays and had a .585 slugging percentage at one time during that month.

Mike admitted that he was pressing too much in the opening series in Cleveland and learned to settle down and be patient. He was chasing pitches out of the strike zone.[vii] It is understandable. Big moments can sometimes lead you to want to make too much happen too soon. However, the best advice is to just be calm, be patient, and relax. Hitters go through slumps and stay in slumps because they try to force the issue. They do not wait for the right pitches. Mike started to illustrate more patience as May came around, and began hitting the ball better and farther.

Believe it or not, Mike did not feel like he had a great May, despite ending the month at .303 with 5 home runs, 6 stolen bases, and 21 runs. For most, that would have been a great rookie month. For Mike, it was nothing compared to what he was capable of. But that full potential was on display in June.

On June 1st against the Rangers, Mike went 2-for-4 with a triple and 3 RBIs. The next night, he went 2-for-4 with a double. Then it was 2-for-5 with another RBI. Then 4-for-4 with a double, run, and RBI. This torrid pace continued throughout the month. He was being started nightly and by mid-June, Trout was hitting .354. The press started to notice what was happening. Who was this kid that came up just barely a month ago and was crushing the baseball? Those who knew Mike were not surprised. This is what they expected.

In July, Mike Trout was invited to play for the American League in the All-Star Game in Kansas City. "It's awesome getting picked. I'm getting chills right now," Trout said at the time, reflecting on the honor. "It's what I always dreamed of as a kid."[xix] Mike's high school coaches, as well as his family and friends from high school, all attended the game. Despite the American League losing 8-0, Mike had a stellar game. He went 1-for-1 with a walk and a stolen base.[xx] Not bad for your first All-Star game. And there would be plenty more to follow.

As the season continued, Mike continued to hammer the ball. He ended his rookie season hitting .326 with 30 home runs and 83 RBIs.[i] He led the league in batting average, stolen bases (49), and runs (129). It was one of the greatest rookie seasons ever in the game. It was so great, Mike Trout was being talked about as being the third player ever in the game to win the Rookie of the Year and MVP in the same season. Ichiro Suzuki and Fred Lynn were the only other two to achieve the honor.[xxv]

Additionally, Mike became the first rookie to join the 30-for-30 Club, hitting 30 home runs and achieving more than 40 stolen bases.[iv] However, while he cruised to AL Rookie of the Year, he came up just short of Miguel Cabrera in the MVP voting.

In just a year, Mike had gained the respect of the team. He was not just another regular rookie looking to find a place with the team. He had his place, and he was impressing even some of the legends of the game.

"No matter the success that he got, the kid just comes in and plays and part of that, too, is that he doesn't have any pressure," 2001 Rookie of the Year winner and teammate Albert Pujols said on describing Trout. "He comes here, he plays around, he acts like a veteran guy, and that's something that veteran guys allow him to do. He belongs here, he knows that, and I think that's something that is really important to him."[xxxviii]

Sophomore Surge

Mike's rookie season was nothing short of sensational. But he didn't want to prove it was a fluke. Many rookies have the tendency to undergo a "Sophomore Slump" season in which their numbers do not reflect their rookie season. They get big heads, thinking success would automatically come to them and they would get better, and then they get a rude awakening.

But Mike was not one to let his head get in the way. That was not the way he was taught by his parents or coaches growing up. Mike knew in order to get better, you had to work for it. Success was not going to come to you, especially in baseball, as hard of a game as it is. Never take anything granted and always give 110% every day. That was the Mike Trout Way.

Mike's goal his second season was simple: Keep getting better.

Mike Trout started his 2013 campaign on a six-game hitting streak and had nine multi-hit games in his first 17. Anyone thoughts he might go into a sophomore slump were quickly dismissed. Trout was slugging over .500 in his first month and getting on base more than anyone in baseball. On May 21, 2013, Mike had one of the best games of his career when he became the youngest player in history to hit for the cycle, doing it at 21 years, 287 days old.[iv] In that game, he went 4-for-5 and drove in 5 runs in helping the Angels to a 12-0 win over the Mariners. By mid-season, he was up near the top of the league in hitting, stolen bases, and slugging percentage and was picked for his second straight All-Star Game.

Mike continued hitting after the All-Star break and was up near the top in every category again. He finished 4th in batting average at .323, third in on-base percentage, and fourth in slugging percentage, but led the American League in runs scored (109). He also led the league in runs created (155), wins above replacement (WAR) (8.9), and situational wins (7.3).[i]

However, Miguel Cabrera continued to stay a step ahead of him in the MVP race. Cabrera led the league in batting, on-base percentage, slugging percentage, and was second in home runs. Cabrera won his second straight AL MVP Award, while Trout finished second once again.

All-Star Machine

By 2014 and 2015, Mike was a regular and automatic pick for the All-Star teams. The 2014 game would be his third straight since his rookie season. It would also be his best.

The 2014 game was notorious for being the final sendoff for Trout's childhood hero, Derek Jeter, who was honored at the game in Minneapolis. Trout started the game in the outfield and made an impact from his first at-bat.

Trout went for 2-for-3 in the game with a double and a triple. He totaled a run with 2 RBIs in helping lead the American League to a 5-3 over the National League. Trout was named the All-Star Game Most Valuable Player as a result of his performance. At 22 years old, Trout became the second-youngest All-Star MVP in history, behind only Ken Griffey, Jr.[xxi]

In 2015, Cincinnati was the host city and once again, Trout delivered another amazing performance. In his first at-bat of the night, Trout homered off Diamondback and National League ace Zack Greinke. The home run was significant because it meant Trout had hit for the natural cycle in his first four All-Star games, something never accomplished before in a player's first four appearances.[xxii]

Trout finished the game with two runs and a walk to go along with his home run and ended up winning the All-Star game MVP yet again. He became the first player in Major League Baseball history not just to hit for the natural cycle in his first four All-Star games, but also to win back-to-back All-Star Game MVPs.[xxii]

Trout's Rise to Fame

In 2014, Trout had enough of finishing runner-up to Miguel Cabrera in the MVP race. It was time to showcase to all of baseball he was the best in the game. He found a way to hit a new level of greatness.

Trout once again led the league in runs (115) and he also would end up leading the league in RBIs (111). While his batting average lowered a bit to .287, he added more power, hitting 36 home runs, his most to date, and had a slugging percentage of .561. He was the unanimous pick for American League MVP.[i]

In 2015, Trout's power numbers continued to escalate. He hit 41 homers and led the league with a .590 slugging percentage. He also led the league with a .991 on-base percentage (OBP). For the second year in a row, however, he finished just shy of .300 and received his third AL MVP Runner-Up, coming up just behind Josh Donaldson. For the fourth year in a row, however, he earned a Silver Slugger Award, an honor he has gone on to earn every single season but one— 2017, when he spent two months on the Disabled List—in Major League Baseball from his rookie season to present-day 2019.[i]

Trout's best year may have been in 2016, however. The slugger was back among the best in hitting, finishing with a batting average of .317, and once again leading all of baseball with 123 runs scored. He posted his second 100+ RBI season and led the league with 116 walks. Trout was named American League MVP for the second time, this time beating out Mookie Betts and Jose Altuve for the honor.[i]

Before May 28, 2017, Trout was enjoying one of his best starts to any season. He was hitting .337 with a .461 on-base percentage and had already belted 16 home runs. He was also leading the league in slugging by a mile at .742. Unfortunately, the rest of the team was hitting .226, which led to the Angels sitting just a game below .500. But his season changed with one stolen base. Diving headfirst into second base, Trout stood up and was wincing in pain. Trout ended up tearing a ligament in his thumb, and before you know it, he was on the disabled list for two months.[xxiii]

The Angels were able to rally around Mike's injury and stay close to .500 while he was gone, finishing the season second in the division. Trout came back and continued to pound the ball. He finished the year first in slugging percentage and on-base percentage. He still somehow managed to finish fourth in voting for the American League MVP despite missing one-third of the season.

By the end of the 2017 season, Mike Trout had established himself as the best in the game. He was now the model athlete, and his story began to spread more and more. He became an inspiration and favorite among little leaguers out there who wanted to be like the Angels rising star. During the Little League World Series, when asked who their favorite player was, most kids said "Mike Trout." And why not? Not only was his play the best among any baseball player their first six seasons in the league, but his humility and respect that he had for others and the game was something that any young athlete would want to replicate.

The 2018 and 2019 season was more of the same for Mike. By his standards, 2018 was not his strongest year, although he did hit 39 home runs and finished with a .312 batting average. It is amazing that this would be considered a subpar season for a baseball player. Plus, he was again hampered by an injury that put him on the disabled list, once again stealing a base and this time hurting his wrist.[xxiv] For the fourth time, Trout finished runner-up in the AL MVP voting, this time behind Mookie Betts of the Red Sox, who helped win his team the World Series.[i]

In 2019, Mike Trout was at his best. He had a career-high 45 home runs, had his third 100+ RBI season and added in 110 runs. Despite only hitting .291, he had a career-high and league-leading .645 slugging percentage and .438 OBP. Trout won his third American League MVP Award, edging out Alex Bregman of the Houston Astros.[i]

Trout's greatness continues to amaze everyone. His WAR of 61.1 has only been topped by two other players in history who have had a higher number after their first eight seasons, Ted Williams and Albert Pujols.[xv]

While some players get stressed and tired of all the work and grind of every day and every season, Mike Trout is the opposite. To him, baseball is freedom. It is entertaining. It is something to put a smile on your face. It is his attitude as well as his amazing talent that has helped inspire so many young athletes.

"The best part of hitting? You have control of what you're doing," Trout told sportswriter Tom Verducci. "It's your box. I love hitting. You put in all the time and practice to go out there and put up good numbers, and it's so fun. I enjoy it so much."[xv]

While some may be confused by that and say the pitcher is the one in control, Trout disagrees. "I flip it. It's your zone. You have to go into that box and own it. Think positive, and it's yours. Don't give the pitcher any advantage to think that it may be his."[xv]

As mentioned already, confidence is such an important part of the game, and part of that confidence is feeling like you own the pitcher and the batter's box. If you let the pitcher control you, then you are playing by their rules. Mike Trout isn't like that. He is setting the example to make the pitcher play by his rules.

Besides his three American League MVP awards, two All-Star MVP awards, and all his Silver Slugger awards, Trout has won the Hank Aaron Award twice

(2014 and 2019), the Player of the Month Award five times, the Wilson Defensive Player of the Year (2012), the Baseball America Player of the Year four times (2012, 2013, 2016, 2018), the Sporting News Player of the Year (2019), and the Esurance Major League Award (2016).[xxv]

"Most baseball speedsters are like Ferraris," according to J.J. Cooper of *Baseball America* who saw Mike Trout play in 2011. "They're small, compact and built to go from home to first in the blink of an eye. But watching Trout was like watching a massive Mercedes with a big engine under the hood. He looked like a power hitter, but when you pulled out the stopwatch, you realized he was faster than all those Ferraris."[xxv]

Chapter 5: Personal Life

Love Life

"I met her in high school, and we trust each other, and she is one of my best friends. She is somebody I can talk to and is always here for me."[xxvi] – *Mike Trout on wife, Jessica Cox Trout,* Philadelphia Daily News

They were high school sweethearts, meeting at Millville High School during their sophomore year. Some may say "love at first sight" is just a myth, but for Mike and Jessica Cox Trout, it was anything but.

Most baseball players will meet what they think is "the girl of their dreams" in high school, but once they achieve stardom, they meet many girls "of their dreams," occasionally for one night. That was not Mike Trout, though. When he was stung by the love bug in high school, he was stung forever. He didn't need to consider any other women or let stardom bring women his way. He was committed from the start. Jessica was his girl from the very beginning.

The two of them dated throughout high school, through Mike's minor league success, and into his major league days. She was by his side from day one through the trials and tribulations, despite living in New Jersey while he was making his way up the ranks in the game. The two have had great companionship, with Jessica being there for Mike before baseball and throughout the whole journey. Many say you should not get married too young, but when you know you have found the right one and have been dating for 11 years, it is time to make the ultimate commitment.[xxviii]

On July 2, 2016, the biggest day of Mike's life came, and it had nothing to do with baseball. Jessica Cox looked up to the sky and saw a message that a plane had written in smoke.[xxvi]

"Will you marry me, Jess?"

Of course, Jessica said yes. They married on December 19, 2017, in a winter-themed wedding that looked something like out of the movie *Frozen*.

Jessica isn't a model or celebrity movie star like you've seen Alex Rodriguez, Derek Jeter, and other baseball stars get involved with. Rather, Jessica is a middle-school teacher in New Jersey. The best part about her job is getting summers off so she can spend them in California watching her husband play baseball. Jessica loves to travel, and with Mike, she gets to do plenty of it.[xxvi]

The two share a lot in common. They love dogs to death and even have an Eskimo dog, Juno, that they regularly share posts about on Instagram and Twitter.[xxvii] The two of them also love giving back to the community and have participated in a variety of charity functions aimed at helping the less fortunate as well as local organizations. One of the charities they take part in is Fill the Boot, which raises money for fire departments throughout the Los Angeles area. They've also worked hard to raise funds for the Special Olympics in Los Angeles.[xxvii]

On March 2, 2020, Mike and Jessica announced that they are expecting their first child. A video was posted on Twitter that showed Jessica stunning Mike with the news. The baby is due in August 2020.

On Twitter, Mike posted to his unborn child, "I don't even know where to begin...from seeing your heartbeat for the first time to seeing you dance around in mommy's belly...we are truly blessed and this is only the beginning." In another post, Mike added, "Little man, you have the best mommy already and I can't wait to be your dad! We are so humbled by this gift God has given us. We love you already, buddy."[xxix]

Most any athlete will tell you that family comes first in life, and having your first child is reason for baseball to take a backseat. Mike appreciates and knows that, and everyone should. It is a special moment in life to not just get married, but have that first child. Appreciate that moment and appreciate that child more than anything; yes, even more than baseball.

Mike has done it the right way. His family taught him the value of loyalty and respect, and he has shown that to his wife, Jessica, since the day they met. While other ballplayers spend their offseasons partying and picking up women, Mike spends them making new memories with his wife and dog, Juno, and will soon be sharing it with their newborn child.

Hobbies and Interests

Many know the baseball side of Mike Trout, but there are a lot of other parts to him, some of them quirky, that you may not know. For example, besides having a love for baseball and animals, Mike has a unique love for the weather. In fact, he calls himself a "weather geek" and wants to be a meteorologist after he retires from baseball. Mike has a separate folder on his phone called "Weather" where he stores all of his weather apps, which totals quite a few.[xxx]

Like many other athletes, Mike is into other sports as well. Growing up, he played basketball at Millville and excelled at it, but surprisingly, it would not be his chosen sport should he suddenly quit baseball. "If I was a professional athlete in another sport, it would have to be golf," Mike admitted to *Fox Sports*. "I try to play daily in the offseason. I'm like a seven or eight, maybe nine handicap. If I don't play every day, then I'm a little shaky."[xxxi]

Trout's dream is to one day play at the Augusta National Golf Club, the home of the Masters Tournament, and with his fame and stardom rising, there is a good chance that Augusta National officials will allow him to step onto the grounds and swing a club. It may not be The Masters, but at least it would be fun. He is a huge fan already of Scottsdale golf courses and once played TPC Scottsdale, where the Phoenix Open is held every year. He also wants to go to Monterrey and play at historic Pebble Beach, which hosts the National Pro-Am every year and the U.S. Open once a decade.[xxxi]

Mike's love for golf is a tribute to what his parents taught him and a lesson for all young athletes to just have fun with life. Do not let what you do for a living completely control you—there needs to be time to smile and enjoy the other perks of living.

As far as food goes, when Mike is on the road, he does not spend much time trying to decide where to eat. It is one place and one place only: Subway. And it is always the same two sandwiches Mike sticks with: Italian on white and Chicken Teriyaki on herb and cheese bread. Mike became such a Subway superstar that he signed a deal with them along with SuperPretzel.[xxxi] Mike also has a deal with Nike which allows the company to sell his branded shoes to young athletes. Along with Nike, he is also an investor and partner in the sports drink company, Bodyarmor SuperDrink.

As Mike's fame continues to rise, he will likely continue to invest in more companies and sign more endorsement deals in the years ahead.

As for music, one of Mike's most famous quotes comes about Bruce Springsteen, a man who grew up not too far from Mike in Asbury Park, New Jersey. Just a guess, but he probably was not a huge fan of the movie *Blinded by the Light*. "Honestly, I'm not really a big Springsteen guy," Mike said. "I'll listen to the music, but...I didn't really get attached to it as much as, like, country artists. That's really who I listen to."[xxxviii]

Any Angels player will tell you that they know Mike's choice of music. Why? He sings it in the shower all the time and can be heard singing it from the locker room. While he also listens to hip hop and R&B (to fire him up before a game, his walk-up songs have ranged anywhere from "Panda" to "All the Way Up"), country music is where his passion lies. In fact, if you follow him on Twitter, you are probably well aware of his music, as he tweets about his country music passions a lot and comments on some of his favorite songs and albums.[xxxi]

The Jokester

"He definitely likes his jokes. That's how he is. Laid-back, likes to have fun; a funny, really nice person."[xxxii] - Ron Tobolski, high school teammate at Millville H.S.

Mike Trout's personality is one of a kind. He may be serious on the field, but off of it, he can be anything but at times. He lives on pranks and sarcasm and can be your everyday comedian. In fact, if there was a movie about his life, he knows just the perfect actor to play it: Adam Sandler. According to Trout, if his life were a movie, Sandler would be the perfect actor to play him. He is a huge fan of his and loves his movies and finds a lot of similarities in terms of their sarcastic nature.[xxxi]

Mike's sense of humor goes all the way back to his childhood and carried with him through the minor leagues and into the majors. Now an established player on the Angels, Mike loves to have fun with the new guys. Call it a bit of the Mike Trout initiation.

One of those new guys who got pranked was Jo Adell, one of the Angels' top prospects. After a spring training workout in 2018, Trout was in the clubhouse shower and motioned to Adell that one of the showerheads was open. Trout then disappeared to towel off. Adell used the showerhead Trout told him was open and before he knew it, the jet stream became so blazing hot you could hear screams from outside the locker room. Adell suddenly heard a toilet flush around the corner and saw Trout peeking around the corner, bawling with laughter.

Who could have pulled such a crazy prank?

When Philadelphia Eagles quarterback and Trout's friend Carson Wentz was asked by the *Bleacher*

Report if Mike was behind it all, Wentz admitted, "That sounds just like 'Philly Mike'. I can see that for sure."[xxxii]

"I use that shower all the time, so it's more me getting caught on accident," Trout said with a guilty smile.

This is the same guy who played jokes on his grandmother growing up. When you are a prankster as a kid, it never leaves you. Every day is April Fool's Day.

Mike's sarcastic and laid-back personality reflects who he is. He is not one for the fancy, lathered-up parties you see some athletes take part in. Mike would rather hang out with his buddies at a bar "on the town" or in the hotel and just tell stories and jokes all night. He is your regular guy. He loves fantasy football, NCAA tournament pools, and shooting baskets in the clubhouse. Of course, it is not just for fun. Mike is very competitive. He wants to win.

"He reminds me a lot of Deter Jeter," Angels general manager Billy Eppler said, a former executive with the New York Yankees. "Their personalities are so similar. Nothing seems to bother them."[xxxii]

If you are looking for a sharp contrast with somebody, maybe a player like Bryce Harper or Manny Machado. Guys that look for the spotlight and worship the fame. Mike is in the spotlight, but it is not because he wants it. It is because it has come to him. He just accepts it. When asked if he would ever push to move back east and leave the Angels for a bigger payday and a life closer to home, Mike basically says, whatever happens, will happen. He enjoys going back to his hometown to see his buddies and family, especially when life gets crazy. The tough part about baseball is the traveling and being away from home so much. But like Mike says, "It is what it is."[xxxii]

According to Angels television analyst Mark Gubicza, whenever Mike does go home, it is like Mick Jagger walking around. He goes to Eagles games a lot to see his buddy Wentz and watch his favorite childhood football team play. It is pretty easy to spot Mike at games. He is the big, athletic guy with a smile on his face all the time.

Gubicza has become friends with Mike over the years, even going to Eagles games with him. Gubicza says that Mike is such an easy guy to get along with, and what you see is what you get. Sometimes you can get too carried away talking with him. People love him. They love being around positive people, and Mike is that way all the time. It is why so many young athletes look up to Mike now. Even the stars do. Wentz and tight end Zac Ertz went out of their way before a game, leaving their pre-game warm-ups just so they could say hi to Mike.

"He brings out the best in you," Ertz said. "You want to be around happy people like that. People that can put a smile on your face. There's not many who can accomplish that more than Mike Trout."[xxxii]

"The guy is living a different life now, but he's still the same guy," Wentz added. "He's not coming to Eagles games with these rich and famous celebrities. He's coming with his high school buddies. And he's so supportive of the Eagles. He's given us shoes and supports the team all the time on social media. It's pretty cool."[xxxiii]

Yes, what you see is truly what you get with Mike Trout. And it is a lesson to every little leaguer out there who is looking for a major leaguer to idolize and look up to. Do not stop being who you are just because you are famous. Be the same person every day of your life. Just accept stardom as a gift; do not let it change who you are or your personality.

Chapter 6: Legacy and Future

There are few safe bets in life, but there is one bet you can bank on without even a question in your mind: Mike Trout is a Hall-of-Famer. The star's list of accomplishments would get him in on the first ballot if he were to retire today. From wins above replacement to MVP honors and contributions on and off the field, Mike Trout has already created a legacy that will live in baseball history for years to come, and every day he plays, the story just gets better.

Trout's 72 WAR is incredible and is ranked right up there with Ty Cobb and Mickey Mantle as players to have this many WAR this early in their careers. Since 2012, the next closest player to Trout is Josh Donaldson at 43 wins above replacement.[xxxiii] Even more incredible, he shares that number of 72 WAR with his childhood hero, Derek Jeter, who needed 20 years to get there.[xxxiii]

His jersey is the highest-selling one in baseball. Since 2012, he ranks third in total walks, second in intentional walks, first in total runs, third in total batting average, second in on-base percentage, and second in slugging percentage.[xxxiii]

However, while all those numbers are great and all of Trout's success is unfathomable at this young an age, baseball is a team game, and in the end, there is something Trout does not have that he would love to hold up one day... A World Series trophy.

World Series championships helped define careers like Derek Jeter's and Reggie Jackson's. They give you the chance to showcase your talents on the biggest stage in baseball and under the most intense pressure. However, the Angels have just not been able to build a championship team around Mike Trout since his arrival. The last time they made a Championship series, Trout was a freshman at Millville High School (2005). The one time the Angels did make the postseason as a wild-card team during Trout's career, they were quickly disposed of in three games.

Some thought Trout would explore free agency like other young stars have recently done, such as Bryce Harper and Giancarlo Stanton, but Trout put an end to that last year, signing a 12-year, $430 million contract with the Angels, the largest contract in pro sports at the time.[xxxiv] Now, the question is, can the Angels build a championship team around him?

The Angels made the first big step in wanting to win one by hiring Joe Maddon to be their manager. Maddon was with the Angels as an assistant when they won the World Series in 2001 and took the Tampa Bay Rays to the World Series in 2008 with the lowest payroll in baseball. He then went to the Chicago Cubs and ended the 108-year drought, winning a World Series for the city.

The Angels have a great farm system, and also recently won the rights to Shohei Ohtani, who is still building up his superstar resume. They also acquired Anthony Rendon, who helped the Washington Nationals win the World Series in 2019.[xxxv]

The Role Model

As time goes on, more and more stories about Mike Trout's impact on the younger population uplift the heart and bring a smile to millions of fans.

There is the story of Mike Trout granting a wish to a young 6th grader named Brody. Like Mike, his favorite team was not the same one as his idol; he was an Astros fan who wanted to be like Mike Trout when he grew up. Brody was so excited, and his mom wanted to share that excitement with Mike Trout, tagging him in the video she posted of herself explaining how much her son loves baseball and looks up to him.[xli] Trout responded on game day at Minute Maid Park, meeting young Brody in the locker room before the game. He gave Brody a signed jersey and a big hug, footage of which made its rounds on social media. Brody's mom posted the videos and the experience and shared just how great it was for Brody all because Mike was such a "stand-up guy."[xli]

There is the story of young Michael, a Kids Wish patient who was born with hydrocephalus and Chiari malformation.[xlii] Michael had already undergone seven brain surgeries along with other procedures. His only happiness in life, he said, was watching the Los Angeles Angels and his favorite player, Mike Trout. Michael got his wish when he got VIP tickets to an Angels home game. He talked to some of the Angels players before the game and even swung some practice swings with Albert Pujols. And then his real dream came true. He came face-to-face with his hero, Mike Trout.

Mike didn't disappoint. He came over and signed every favorite item of young Michael's, bringing the biggest smile to his face. He signed so many of Michael's items, they would last a lifetime. The two spent time talking and took pictures together. The moment made young Michael's life.[xlii] "Michael's in better spirits since his wish and made great memories," Michael's mom, Crystal, said of the experience.[xlii]

And then there is the story of Jaylon Fong, a 14-year old leukemia survivor who played for West Covina Little League. Fong was invited to an Angels game and spent some time on the field socializing with some of the Angels players. A week later, while practicing with his teammates on the little league, out of nowhere, Jaylon's idol Mike Trout showed up. Trout spoke to the team and gave them tips on how to handle themselves and move forward in the game and in life. Mike gave them a speech about how he was in the same spot they were and gave them many of the same words of wisdom that his parents gave him as a kid which led to his success: Stay out of trouble, be a good kid, be respectful, and practice. Do that, and good things would come their way.[xliii]

After that, Mike spent some private time with Jaylon. The two shared stories together, and then Jaylon handed Mike Trout a courage bracelet. When Jaylon watched the Angels game that night, Mike was wearing it.

There are dozens more stories like this, and, no doubt, dozens more to come in the future. Mike Trout has a special spot in his heart for those who battle a much larger fight than the tribulations of baseball. Baseball is just a game, but for these kids, what they go through is so much more. Mike wants them to know he is there for them and always supporting them. It is who he is. It is who we all should be. The world would be a better place if there were more Mike Trouts out there— athletes that put others first in their hearts and appreciate their fight, which is so much harder than their own.

Mike wants kids to grow up like he did, enjoying the game and enjoying life. Practicing not so much because they *have* to, but practicing because they *want* to. Having that drive inside to get better and be a star one day.

You Do Not Cheat to Win

Mike Trout has already been identified as a jokester, a straight arrow, a competitive machine, and a true gentleman. His fun, laid-back attitude is what separates him from almost every other ballplayer. However, while Mike is one of the easiest guys to get along with and one that people enjoy being around, he has no patience or room whatsoever when it comes to cheating.

In the winter of 2020, the Houston Astros were caught stealing signs from other teams and using those signs to benefit their offense as they made World Series runs in the late 2010s, even winning it in 2017. While many baseball players stayed quiet on the sign-stealing scandal concerning the Astros, Trout spoke up, citing the importance of protecting the future of our game and how the Astros had dishonored that by their actions.

"It's sad for baseball," Trout told ABC News' Alden Gonzalez. "It's tough. They cheated. I don't agree with the punishments, the players not getting anything. It was a player-driven thing. It sucks, too, because guys' careers have been affected, a lot of people lost jobs. Me going up to the plate knowing what was coming— it would be pretty fun up there."[xxxvi]

Mike always knew something was fishy with the team, citing he noticed they would bang the bat to indicate a sign and they just never missed a pitch. He says he lost a lot of respect for many of the guys he knows and that it was tough to see for the game.[xxxvi]

Trout has never been involved in a scandal in an age when baseball is anything but scandal-free. He has stayed clean and clear of steroids and other performance-enhancing drugs and built his reputation with his bat and personality. Mike wants to help not just his reputation, but baseball's as well.

"We don't need cheating in the game," Mike said. "There's no place for it. We need to set good examples for the kids growing up watching us play. Stuff like this (the Astros scandal) is damaging to the sport."[xxxvi]

As Mike Trout enters the prime of his career, he is stepping up as a leader for not just his team, the Angels, but all of baseball. He wants to help make baseball a sport that people look up to again instead of one that is constantly shrouded in scandal like it has been for the last 25 years.

Showing Quiet Leadership

Baseball is a game that is looking for people to step up to the plate, not literally but figuratively. It is looking for good examples so our youngest generation can learn to love the game and appreciate it. It is looking for players to never take a play off, to give 100% effort every second of every game. It is looking for leadership.

Mike Trout isn't the most outspoken guy in the game. He isn't one to give interviews at every turn or frequently make his opinion known on controversial subjects. He does not speak out against others on his team or voice his displeasures in an effort to bring down his team. Instead, Mike lets his bat and personality do the talking.

So how does Mike Trout want to illustrate leadership?

1. Show Positive Thinking

"When you get into that box, you have to go in there and own it," Trout says. "Think positive and it's yours. Control what you're doing. It's your box. Own it."[xxxvii]

Trout has done this. The word "slump" does not really come to mind when you think of Trout. Not when you look at his batting averages since his rookie season and his wins above replacement. His positive nature has not just helped him off the field, but it has helped him at the plate and in the field.

2. Keep it Simple

"You can't ever let failure ever enter your mind," Trout says. "Complexity is often the enemy of success. My philosophy is 'Keep it Simple.' I think too much information for me is bad. Less is more for me. That's why I call timeout a lot. If I'm in the box and start thinking, I've got to clear my mind. Reset mode."[xxxvii]

Mike does not just say this, he shows it. He walks a lot because he does not press the issue and think too much. He smiles all the time because he does not let the bad things going around him get him down. He hits so well because he does not let his head get in the way. He just goes about his business.

3. Show Consistency

Being consistent and faithful are the foundations of a strong leader's success, according to Angels bench coach Dino Ebel. You never change and bring the same attitude, the same hard work, and the same leadership to the park every day. "He never changes who he is," Abel said.[xxxvii]

Mike Trout has so many examples in life of being a leopard that does not change his spots. Every time you look for a reason to not like him, you come up empty. Every time you look for something that shows he is different than what you see, you fail. You'll never find Mike changing his level of play night in and night out. He is consistent. He brings the same attitude, the same work ethic, the same hunger and competitiveness to the ballpark every single day. It never changes.

4. Show Progression

Mike Trout's goal is very simple: to get better every day. There is no limit.

The best leaders know there is no such thing as reaching the peak of the mountain. The best leaders set small goals, reach them, and then set new goals.

Trout's was always to get better, no matter what. Some players reach their peak and are happy with that and gloat about it. Not Mike. It is always "What can I do to get better?" No matter how much you achieve, try to achieve more.

5. Be Resilient

A bad mood? Not Mike Trout. Those that know Mike best have made comments about how, even on days when he goes 0-for-4, he does not let it get him down. He stays positive and learns from it.[xxxvii]

Inside, Trout will obviously be disappointed if he has a bad game, but he is not one to show it and let it linger. He does not allow temporary setbacks to be permanent. He just tells himself to go back out there the next night and do better.

Kids can learn a lot from Mike Trout. From his humility to his resiliency to his consistency. The man leads by example, and it is up to the younger generation to follow him and in his footsteps. He is the ideal athlete to mimic and want to be. Learn the lessons from him and you have a great life in the future.

Conclusion

"He is something different. He is a throwback, there's no question about it. What I'm probably more proud of with Mike (Trout) is his modesty. His character. He understands he's a man playing a kid's game. He's doing what he's wanted to do all his life. And love it." xxxviii *– Mayor Shannon in an interview with the* Los Angeles Times

The quote from Shannon really describes who Mike Trout is best. He is living the dream in a way that is not changing him. The humble side of Mike...the respectful side of Mike...the humorous side of Mike...the laid-back side of Mike...it hasn't changed one bit since he was a young boy growing up in a middle-class New Jersey neighborhood. The only thing that has changed is that he has become better at hitting a baseball and has become more mature with age.

With Trout's latest contract, it is likely he finishes his career with the Angels and becomes an easy first-ballot Hall-of-Famer. He will stride to break more records and make his own place in history. He hopes to add a world series ring to his hand and help be a mentor to future Angels who join the organization. With the strong farm system the team has, it is likely he will be doing a lot of mentoring.

If there is one piece of advice that baseball can take away in today's day and age it is that the game needs more people and players like Mike Trout. Players who put others first in their life. Players who stay committed to who they are. Players who take their parents' stellar advice and use it when they are older. Players who show respect, humility, and grace to others. Players who stand as the perfect role model to teenagers out there and give them reasons to say, "I want to be like Mike." Players who truly define what baseball and life should be about.

Everyone should know Mike Trout's story. Once you know it, it will make you want to be a better person. It will make you look at the game in a better light. It will make you forget all the bad things in the world and instead, look at the good. It will give you hope that baseball is truly headed in the right direction.

Mike Trout is a game-changer. The more kids that try to be like him, the more they will change the game for the better.

Final Word/About the Author

I was born and raised in Norwalk, Connecticut. Growing up, I could often be found spending many nights watching basketball, soccer, and football matches with my father in the family living room. I love sports and everything that sports can embody. I believe that sports are one of most genuine forms of competition, heart, and determination. I write my works to learn more about influential athletes in the hopes that from my writing, you the reader can walk away inspired to put in an equal if not greater amount of hard work and perseverance to pursue your goals. If you enjoyed *Mike Trout: The Inspiring Story of One of Baseball's All-Stars,* please leave a review! Also, you can read more of my works on *Serena Williams, Rafael Nadal, Roger Federer, Novak Djokovic, Richard Sherman, Andrew Luck, Rob Gronkowski, Brett Favre, Calvin Johnson, Drew Brees, J.J. Watt, Colin Kaepernick, Aaron Rodgers, Peyton Manning, Tom Brady, Russell Wilson, Gregg Popovich, Pat*

Riley, John Wooden, Steve Kerr, Brad Stevens, Red Auerbach, Doc Rivers, Erik Spoelstra, Michael Jordan, LeBron James, Kyrie Irving, Klay Thompson, Stephen Curry, Kevin Durant, Russell Westbrook, Anthony Davis, Chris Paul, Blake Griffin, Kobe Bryant, Joakim Noah, Scottie Pippen, Carmelo Anthony, Kevin Love, Grant Hill, Tracy McGrady, Vince Carter, Patrick Ewing, Karl Malone, Tony Parker, Allen Iverson, Hakeem Olajuwon, Reggie Miller, Michael Carter-Williams, John Wall, James Harden, Tim Duncan, Steve Nash, Draymond Green, Kawhi Leonard, Dwyane Wade, Ray Allen, Pau Gasol, Dirk Nowitzki, Jimmy Butler, Paul Pierce, Manu Ginobili, Pete Maravich, Larry Bird, Kyle Lowry, Jason Kidd, David Robinson, LaMarcus Aldridge, Derrick Rose, Paul George, Kevin Garnett, Chris Paul, Marc Gasol, Yao Ming, Al Horford, Amar'e Stoudemire, DeMar DeRozan, Isaiah Thomas, Kemba Walker, Chris Bosh, Andre Drummond, JJ Redick, DeMarcus Cousins, Wilt Chamberlain, Bradley Beal,

Rudy Gobert, Aaron Gordon, Kristaps Porzingis, Nikola Vucevic, Andre Iguodala, Devin Booker, John Stockton, Jeremy Lin, Chris Paul, Pascal Siakam, Jayson Tatum, Gordon Hayward, Nikola Jokic, Bill Russell, Victor Oladipo, Luka Doncic, Ben Simmons, Shaquille O'Neal, Joel Embiid, Donovan Mitchell, Damian Lillard and Giannis Antetokounmpo in the Kindle Store. If you love baseball, check out my website at claytongeoffreys.com to join my exclusive list where I let you know about my latest books and give you lots of goodies.

Like what you read? Please leave a review!

I write because I love sharing the stories of influential athletes like Mike Trout with fantastic readers like you. My readers inspire me to write more so please do not hesitate to let me know what you thought by leaving a review! If you love books on life, baseball, or productivity, check out my website at claytongeoffreys.com to join my exclusive list where I let you know about my latest books. Aside from being the first to hear about my latest releases, you can also download a free copy of *33 Life Lessons: Success Principles, Career Advice & Habits of Successful People.* See you there!

Clayton

References

[i] "Mike Trout Stats". *Baseball-Reference*. Nd. Web.

[ii] "What They Say". *JockBio*. 2012. Web.

[iii] "Mike Trout". *The Famous People*. Nd. Web.

[iv] "Mike Trout Biography Facts, Childhood, Career & Personal Life". *StoryTell*. 29 Jul 2019. Web.

[v] Augustyn, Adam. "Mike Trout, American Baseball Player". *Britannica*. 2020. Web.

[vi] Strege, David. "Facts About Mike Trout That May Surprise You". *USA Today*. 13 Aug 2019. Web.

[vii] Miller, Sam. "The Phenom". *ESPN*. 20 Sep 2012. Web.

[viii] Kestin, Todd. "Parenting an All-Star". *HuffPost*. 6 Dec 2017. Web.

[ix] "Mike Trout's Dad's Advice on Raising Young Athletes". *Fatherly*. 08 Jun 2017. Web.

[x] Castro, Esther. "Mike Trout's Baseball Coach Talks About the Kind of Athlete Trout Was". *6abc*. 24 Mar 2019. Web.

[xi] Baumann, Michael. "The Best Player in Baseball Doesn't Want to be a Superstar." *The Ringer*. 20 Mar 2017. Web.

[xii] Olney, Buster. "Inside the Discovery of Mike Trout". ESPN. 29 Jul 2018. Web. 11

[xiii] Townsend, Mike. "Mike Trout Asks Derek Jeter for an Autograph at the Most Awkward Time". *Yahoo Sports*. 29 Jun 2018. Web.

[xiv] DeCock, Luke. "Decock: For ECU's Godwin, Trout's the One That Got Away". *TheNewsObserver*. 23 Aug 2013. Web.

[xv] Verducci, Tom. "The Star That Still Won't Shine. The Incredible, Unprecedented but Unseen Greatness of Mike Trout". *CNN Sports Illustrated*. 12 Jul 2018. Web.

[xvi] "Mike Trout Biography". *JockBio*. ND. Web.

[xvii] Lindberg, Ben. "Solving the Mystery of Mike Trout's First Season". *The Ringer*. 7 Apr 2017. Web.

[xviii] "Rocky Balboa Quotes". *GoodReads*. Nd. Web.

[xix] McGarry, Michael. "Millville's Mike Trout Named American League All-Star in Rookie Season." *The Press of Atlantic City*. 1 Jul 2012. Web.

[xx] "2012 All-Star Game Box Score." *Baseball Reference*. 10 Jul 2012. Web.

[xxi] Axisa, Mike. "Mike Trout Named 2014 All-Star Game MVP." *CBS Sports*. 15 Jul 2014.

[xxii] Clair, Michael. "Mike Trout Continues to be Unreal: "Has Now Hit for the Natural Cycle in His First Four All-Star Games". *MLB.com*. 14 Jul 2015.

[23] Reiter, Ben. "Mike Trout Is Injured, But the Angels Have Only Improved in His Absence". *Sports Illustrated.* 29 Jun 2017. Web.

[24] "Injured Mike Trout Sits Out with Injured Right Wrist." *ESPN.* 2 Aug 2018. Web.

[25] "Mike Trout Awards". *Baseball Almanac.* Nd. Web.

[26] "Mike Trout's Wife Jessica Tara Cox". *Player Wives.* 10 Mar 2020. Web.

[27] Kapusta, Michelle. "Who is Mike Trout's Wife, Jessica Cox?" *Cheat Sheet.* 19 Mar 2019. Web.

[28] Kleinschmidt, Jessica. "Listen to Mike Trout Talk About His Wife and Family and How They Keep Him Grounded." *MLB.com.* 8 Mar 2018. Web.

[29] Zucker, Joseph. "Mike Trout, Wife Jessica Reveal They're Expecting 1st Child." *Bleacher Report.* 2 Mar 2020. Web.

[30] "Mike Trout". *Celebrity Beliefs.* 19 Jul 2018. Web.

[31] "10 Things to Know About Mike Trout". *Fox Sports.* 10 Apr 2013. Web.

[32] Miller, Scott. "Mike Trout is Built for Anaheim, but He is Still Philly's Guy". *Bleacher Report.* 25 Jun 2018. Web.

[33] Feinsand, Mark. "Trout's HS Coach Surprised by His Degree of Success". *MLB.com.* 9 Jun 2017. Web.

[34] Calcaterra, Craig. "Mike Trout's New $430 Million Contract is a Bargain". *NBC Sports.* 2019. Web.

[35] Schoenfield, David. "Five Reasons $430 Man Mike Trout Can Win a World Series with Angels". *ESPN.* 19 Mar 2019. Web.

[36] Gonzalez, Alden. "Angels Star Mike Trout Rips Astros, Calls for More Punishment". *ABC News.* 12 Feb 2020. Web.

[37] Dodd, Brian. "Nine Leadership Lessons and Quotes from Mike Trout - The Best Player in Baseball". *BrianDoddonLeadership.com.* 3 Sep 2018. Web.

[38] "Mike Trout Quotes". *Baseball Almanac.* 08 Feb 2013. Web.

[39] Freidman, Josh. "Mike Trout: The Day He Was Intentionally Walked with the Bases Loaded". *The Courier Post.* 8 May 2018. Web.

[40] Caldwell, Mike. "Millville Slugger: Mike Trout's Monster Season". *NJ Monthly.* 15 Jan 2013. Web.

[41] Lindsley, Amanda. "A Dream Come True: La. Boy Meets Idol Mike Trout". WAFB News. 8 Jul 2019. Web.

[42] "Michael's Wish is a Home Run with the Los Angeles Angels." *Kids Wish Network.* 17 Sep 2019. Web.

[43] "Little League Cancer Survivor Gets to Meet Baseball Idol Mike Trout." *ABC News.* 2015 Aug 2017. Web.

[44] Miller, Jeff. "'Just Mike' Trout is the Angels Leader by Example". Los Angeles Times. 21 Mar 2018. Web.

Made in the USA
Las Vegas, NV
15 November 2020